Kimochis®

Feeling Pillows Guide
for Mental Health Professionals

Congratulations!
You are now the **optimistic** and **hopeful** owner of Kimochis® feeling pillows and this handbook for using them! Inside this guide you will find a whole bunch of powerful and playful communication tools.
But before you start reading or working with clients …

DO THIS ONE THING:

Pour all the Kimochis® feeling pillows onto the floor or a table.
Spend a few minutes sitting with the feelings. Touch them, turn them over to see the expression that goes along with the feeling word.
Notice your own reactions to the various feeling pillows.

When done, put the pillows in a bowl, basket, or vase
and make them a permanent part of your therapy space.

Get **curious**.
Be **brave**.
Feel **proud**.
You are ready to begin.

Enjoy,
Ellen & Jill

Published in the United States by Plushy Feely Corp.,
creators of Kimochis®
kimochis.com

Contents

Introduction

Kimochis® offers a hands-on, playful, and interactive way to help children develop and speak the language of emotion. Using the **Kimochis® feeling pillows** as a therapeutic tool, the activities provided in this guidebook will lead children to expand their feelings vocabulary, learn to better understand themselves, increase their ability to express feelings, and improve their overall communication with others. This series of activities will guide you, the mental health professional, in providing the people you serve with opportunities to:

- Practice experiencing a wide variety of emotions
- Connect to the ways that feelings fuel thoughts that lead to behavior
- Develop ways to help themselves feel better
- Recognize the feelings of others
- Increase compassion for self and others
- Learn how to communicate feelings effectively to others

The *Kimochis® Activity Guide for Mental Health Professionals* brings a combination of compassion and imagination to dealing with feelings. This initial set of activities is geared toward children ages 7–12, but you will see that the activities are readily adaptable for younger children, teens, and adults as well. Manuals, videos, and more for other age groups are in the works at Kimochis® Way. The Kimochis® activities in this guide are grouped by different objectives:

Group 1 activities focus on building a feelings vocabulary.

Group 2 activities examine the physical nature of feelings and their impact on thoughts and behavior.

Group 3 activities explore the importance of talking about feelings.

Group 4 activities look at sharing feelings—how to and with whom.

Together, these tasks impart beliefs that comprise the Kimochis® philosophy, including:

- Feelings are neither good nor bad; it's what you do with them that makes the difference.
- Even big, hard-to-have feelings are important and can be handled in helpful ways.
- Much can be expressed without a lot of speaking but with a lot of good listening.

At their most basic level of usability, the Kimochis® feeling pillows can just be tossed into a basket or bowl in your therapy area, seeing what your clients will spontaneously do with them. This is a "less is more" approach to using the pillows as a therapy tool, and it can lead to some very good interactions.

For more of a structured approach, however, we provide the activities below, which have come about organically through playing with the pillows with our clients and students. By repeating each activity numerous times in different scenarios, we've learned that some work best with certain clients, some with others. Taken together, these activities represent our "home runs" and are meant to guide and also to serve as ideas for stimulating your own imagination and creativity. Although the sections below are ordered in a way that allows for the growth and development of feelings, the activities within each section do not need to be done in any particular order. Do what you believe will be most effective for you and the child(ren) with whom you're working. Combine activities, repeat activities, repeat activities from one section in another, come up with something totally new. There's no limit to how you can apply, adapt, and adjust the activities to yield the greatest impact. Along the way, be sure to acknowledge the changes you observe in the children you work with as they develop their capacity to recognize and express what they feel.

Getting Started the Kimochis® Way

We're sure you're eager to just jump right into the activities, but it's best to begin by entering the Kimochis® mind-set. To do so, we present **Kimochis® 7 Extremely Helpful Ways to Talk About Feelings**—concepts that are fundamental to the Kimochis® approach. You, the therapist, can directly and intentionally teach each concept in your sessions or sprinkle them into your work as you see fit, as they're sprinkled throughout the activities.

1. **Practice.** Practice does not make perfect, but it does make things better and easier. Kimochis® is all about making things better over time. So you will want to repeat these activities over and over in order to provide lots of opportunities to practice and incorporate what's being learned. Say the word "practice" frequently as you direct and repeat activities. Explain that everyone needs to practice in order to learn new things and that practice involves putting in effort and trying again and again. Ultimately, practice is habit-forming.

2. **Habit.** The Kimochis® Way speaks of developing *habits* rather than *skills.* The word "skill" can give the impression that someone either has an ability or does not have that ability. It can also make one think that there is a right and a wrong way to do something. In contrast, consider the word "habit." A habit is often acquired without being directly taught. People can develop not-so-good habits, but with teaching, repetition, practice, positive feedback, coaching, and gentle reminders, people can also learn and form new, positive habits. Using the word "habit" in relation to developing positive communication tools can help kids feel more hopeful that they can learn and improve. It can also encourage children to be more open to redoing or trying again when they forget to use positive communication habits.

3. **Tools.** Talk with the children you're working with about how tools help people. For example, hammers help us build. Pencils help us draw and write. Likewise, communication tools help us make and keep friends, resolve conflict, and do our best in school, at home, and in life. Using the word "tools" during your sessions makes communication sound and feel more tangible and lets children know there are positive actions they can take to express feelings.

4. **Size.** From the very beginning of any conversation about feelings, you can help children make the connection between mind and body by asking them to use their body to show how large their feelings feel. Ask kids to use their arms and hands, feet and legs, to respond to, for example, *"Are you a little mad, medium-sized mad, or really, really big mad?"* Conversely, you might ask, *"Are you feeling a little optimistic, medium-sized optimistic, or really, really big optimistic?"* The Kimochis® activities will focus on this directly in order to help children understand that feelings can be felt in different intensities, can come and go, and can be made more manageable by learning things to say and do to help them feel better. It's important to convey that feelings can be made smaller and bigger depending on whether we want to feel more or less of them.

5. **Story.** Most people start a conversation with the standard "wh" questions: *What? When? Where? Why? How?* Typically, these questions result in simple answers. For instance, when you ask someone, *"How are you?"* most people will reply with *"Fine."* Instead, try asking for a *story* as a way to encourage a fuller, richer response. Ask children to tell you a story about their feeling, thought, and/or experience. Everyone likes a story, and using the word "story" can also help a child feel less interrogated or put on the spot.

   Children can also be taught to tell themselves stories about what they are dealing with, incorporating feeling words, concepts, and tools they're learning into their stories to help them get through a tough experience. This fosters self-talk and helps build resiliency; furthermore, it promotes self-help and self-care that lead to self-confidence.

6. **Mistakes.** Everyone makes mistakes, and that's okay! This is what you want to communicate to the children you work with as they strive to learn about their feelings and how to express them. People may yell or say unkind words in the heat of the moment. The Kimochis® Way understands this and believes that everyone deserves a **redo**—the chance to stop and start again if they make a communication mistake. It's not about changing what is felt but about making another effort to communicate feelings more effectively.

7. **Hard-to-Have Feelings.** Feelings can be put into two basic categories: feelings we like to have and feelings we do not like to have. Explain to children that *all* feelings are important and necessary. All feelings help us to learn and to grow, even the ones that make us feel bad and aren't easy to live with. Feelings are very powerful and can affect how we think and act, and they can make our bodies not feel good on the inside. We label this category of upset feelings

"hard-to-have feelings." Talking about these feelings in this way helps children get some distance from tough emotions. This then allows them to develop ways to deal with these feelings and use communication tools to make things better for both themselves and others.

Now it's time to introduce you to the **Kimochis® 7 Keys to Communication**—the tools that help develop resilience and help people communicate in positive ways.

Refer to these Keys to Communication as you do the activities. Encourage the children you work with to use these keys as they interact and communicate with others. There's also a communication vocabulary for each key, which we call our **Kimochis® Social-Emotional Learning (SEL) Vocabulary** (see Appendix D at the back of this guide).

Key 1: Call the person's name and wait for eye contact before speaking.

Key 2: Use volume and tone of voice in helpful ways.

Key 3: Use facial expressions and body language that are helpful and not hurtful.

Key 4: Use words that help rather than hurt.

Key 5: Take a "redo" when you make a communication mistake.

Key 6: Show kindness and forgiveness by letting others take a redo when they make mistakes.

Key 7: Assume the best in others.

*Note: When you work with kids, you also often work with the adults in their lives. Parents and other caretakers can be a big help in bringing their child along on the emotional development continuum. (We have also seen kids bring Kimochis® learning home to their families!) So the **Kimochis® 7 Extremely Helpful Ways to Talk About Feelings** (Appendix A) and the **Kimochis® 7 Keys to Communication** (Appendix C) are available as handouts at the back of this guide—you can make photocopies of them to display in your office and to distribute to clients so they can hang them at home. We suggest having a session with parents, either alone or with their child, to model integrating these concepts into how they connect with their child. When a child is between the ages of 3 and 6 years (or is functioning at this level), we recommend using the **Kimochis® 5 Keys to Communication** (Appendix B).*

Activity Materials

Most of the activities in this book require minimal, if any, materials beyond the requisite **Kimochis® Mixed Bag of Feelings**, and even then, they're very common items found in most offices or households. You can even make adequate substitutions, as suitable. If you'd like to have all materials on hand before launching into this social-emotional learning project for children, here's what we recommend:

- Container for your Kimochis® feeling pillows (a large basket or bowl is perfect)
- Pencils, pens, crayons, markers
- Paper (regular drawing paper, construction paper, cardstock, cardboard)
- Paper plates (that can be written on)
- Tape
- Roll of ribbon
- Small container with lid
- Clear container with lid
- Various art supplies, as desired: clay, Play-Doh, pipe cleaners
- Balloons
- Sheet of blank stickers (any size will do)
- Kitchen mixing spoon
- Mixing bowl
- Pot (for soup or stew)
- A couple of heavy objects and light objects

Optional:
- Target/bull's-eye poster
- Wide roll of craft paper
- Small scale
- Flat stones or blocks
- Velcro or glue
- Pair of large shoes
- Angry face mask

Group 1: Getting Friendly with Feelings

• • • • • • • • • • • • • • • • • • •

KIMOCHIS® FEELINGS FACT:
There's more to feelings than being just mad, sad, or glad.

Kids (and adults, too) are often quite minimalist when it comes to identifying and relating to their feelings. "Mad," "sad," "glad," "okay," and "fine" are the most commonly expressed feeling words, but we of course know that there are hundreds of other more nuanced feelings, like "annoyed," "upset," "joyful," "irritated," "so-so," and "confused." There is a wide range of feelings to describe reactions we have to the experiences that make up our lives, and our goal in this section of the activity guide is to help kids access and express those feelings. This group of activities therefore focuses on building a **feelings vocabulary**, which will enhance a child's emotional understanding and self-awareness.

•————————————————————•

Therapeutic Objective:
Increase feelings vocabulary, along with the ability to talk more comfortably about feelings.

•————————————————————•

The Activities

Before engaging in any of the activities below, begin by explaining to the child that pretty much everything people do and think involves a feeling. We may or may not know what the feeling is or be aware of it at the time, but we are virtually ALWAYS feeling something. Talk with the child about different situations in which feelings exist but they may not be aware of them, like when lying in bed, sitting on the toilet, playing a computer game. Knowing what we feel is not always *fun,* but it's *fun*damental to helping us be in charge of what we think and how we behave.

We suggest keeping your Kimochis® feeling pillows in a bowl or basket in your therapy room. Interestingly, we have observed that changing the shape, size, and feel of the container often changes how people interact with the pillows. Some container options are: a wide basket (so people can see all the words on the pillows at a glance), a bucket (for digging), a backpack (for unpacking), or a tall glass vase (to point to feelings).

Keep the pillows out so clients can naturally explore, ask questions, and get connected to their feelings. Just seeing and touching the Kimochis® feeling pillows often leads to some crucial conversations that can bring healing and help to the heart.

HELLO FEELINGS! Sit with the child at a table or on the floor. Hand the bowl of feelings to the child and ask them to pour out all the feelings. Spend a few minutes together exploring the pillows, looking at the words and facial expressions that go with them. Observe with them how many different feelings there are and how they are all mixed together. Remind the child that this is how people are too and that a wide variety of feelings are necessary for healing and that all feelings are acceptable. Let the child know that you have many fun activities you'll do together that will help them learn more about their feelings and how to handle them.

WHAT FEELINGS DO YOU KNOW? Gather together a sheet of paper and coloring/writing tools. Begin by writing the title *My Feelings Poster* at the top of the page. Have the child choose something to write with and ask them to write down as many feeling words as they know. For children who do not write yet or don't want to, you can do the writing for them. (Of note is that some people see words in color, so you might ask the child if they see their feelings as being a particular color.)

Next, have the child empty the bowl of Kimochis® feeling pillows onto a table or the floor. Then have them match the words they wrote with the corresponding feeling pillows. Put those feeling pillows in a pile. Next, look at the words on the remaining pillows—the feelings they did *not* write down. Talk about any they may not understand. Once you've explained those feelings to them, add those words to their poster as well. (If there are feelings they listed that don't have a pillow to match, we have an activity for that too—we'll get to it soon!)

Ask the child to become a **"feelings detective"** in between your meetings with them, telling them to listen for new, interesting feeling words and then bring them to your next session. You'll also want to bring some fun new feeling words to your sessions, like "perplexed," "elated," "gob-smacked." Add all the new words to the poster as the child learns and collects more feeling words.

HOW FEELINGS WORK. Acknowledge from the previous activity how many feeling words the child already knows. Explain that feelings, at their simplest, can be put into one of two categories: (1) feelings our body enjoys having and (2) feelings our body does not enjoy having. Share that we call this second group of feelings **"hard-to-have feelings"** as they don't feel good inside us. Explain that all feelings are important, even the difficult ones, because they help us learn and grow.

Get two paper plates. Have the child draw a happy face on one and a sad face on the other. (Or you can create these plates yourself ahead of time.) Ask the child to sort the feeling pillows onto the two plates to show which feelings they enjoy having and which they find hard to have. Help the child as needed. The child may find that some feelings are hard to sort because the way that feeling impacts them depends on the situation that triggers that feeling. For example, you can have a happy surprise or an upsetting surprise. Talk about this. Some children may opt to put some of the pillows between the two plates, which itself can lead to an interesting discussion and important insights.

Let the child know that you will be teaching them communication tools to help them handle hard-to-have feelings so that they can help make things better for themselves and others when faced with challenges. Additionally, let the child know that you will be coaching them to learn ways to create more nice-to-have feelings!

CHARADES. This is an old-fashioned game that is always a big hit. To play, take turns with the child pulling feeling pillows one at a time and acting it out for the other to guess. You can keep score if you want, but this activity is really more about having fun with feelings while simultaneously giving children an opportunity to practice showing how feelings "look" on people and what actions they prompt. Kids like repetition, so you can play this game somewhat regularly—to act out feelings experienced in the past week, for example, or feelings you'd like to have more of. You can also make the activity more verbal by lining up the feeling pillows on the floor word-side-up. Then take turns describing or acting out a situation in which someone might have this feeling. For example, for **sorry**, you could say, "*A person might have this feeling if they accidentally broke their sister's toy.*"

FEELINGS MAKER. There are many, many feelings out there in the world. Your "feelings detective" kids will bring in feelings, and they may also be great at creating them. For example, did you know that "constipated" can be an emotion? Or "hexxy"—the feeling of being happy and excited at the same time? For those feelings that children identify themselves or for which there is currently no corresponding Kimochis® feeling pillow, we've created a **Make Your Own Kimochis® Feelings Template** (see Appendix E at the back of this guide). Print out multiple copies of the pillow shape, cut them out, and then let children write their own feeling words and draw their own facial expressions on them. When you have several, laminate them, trim them as needed, and then add them to your bowl of feelings! This helps kids realize that there are lots of feelings out there and that other kids are working on building their feelings vocabulary too.

Note: Each pack of Kimochis® feeling pillows comes with three blank pillows, because, as we all know, there are way more feelings than there are pillows! Allow the child to discover a blank pillow and express curiosity about it. Explain that there's not always a word for how we are feeling, or we may not feel ready yet to talk about our feelings. You can write a significant new feeling that comes up during one of your sessions on one of the blank pillows, you can let the child do so, or the child can make a cutout of the new feeling instead (see above). Either way, add the new pillow to your feelings bowl as the child's vocabulary grows. And always keep at least one blank pillow for those times when children just don't know what they're feeling or don't have a word(s) to describe it.

FEELING FAMILIAR. Sit with the bowl of feeling pillows in between you and the child. Take turns picking a pillow from the bowl and sharing a time you each felt that feeling. Feelings can be specifically chosen or picked randomly. Practice talking about feelings, and in subsequent sessions, you can each talk about a time you felt that feeling since you last met.

Note: Encourage the child to consider a wide variety of life experiences. If the child uses a feeling word incorrectly or can't identify a feeling, provide an explanation of the appropriate word, along with a situation in which that feeling might be felt. For **insecure**, *for example: "This is a feeling you might have if you are not yet sure about what you are doing or saying. You might feel insecure, or not confident, in a new situation because you are uncertain about how to act. Starting at a new school could make you feel insecure."*

Kids may use the same example to explain two different feelings. Acknowledge that they could feel both feelings in the one situation, but ask them to give an additional example of a time they had or could have the second feeling. If, for instance, the child says they felt **sad** *when their friend didn't include them in a game and then repeats that same situation for the feeling* **left out**, *acknowledge that you would feel both sad and left out in that situation too, but then ask for a different time they felt sad (like when they got sick and couldn't go to a friend's party). This encourages children to really think about their life experiences and their reactions to them.*

WEEKLY HIGHLIGHTS. Invite the child to choose one or more feelings they especially enjoyed having during the week. You can choose one or two feelings as well. Tell each other about the situations that evoked these enjoyable feelings. You can build on this by pulling another feeling from the bowl that is being experienced in the retelling and/or by pulling another feeling the listener is experiencing as the speaker is remembering the feeling. For example, the child may talk about feeling **excited** because school was unexpectedly cancelled one day. Then they might pull **disappointed** because they had to return to school the next day. You, however, could explain that you felt **happy** while listening to the child's excitement and then share a time when you yourself felt excited. This helps children begin to make connections between varied feelings while expanding their capacity for communication about emotions.

QUIET PLEASE. You can make any of the above activities nonverbal for children who find it really hard to talk about their feelings. These children can be encouraged to show rather than tell. Ask these children to show you all the feelings they felt this week. You can add prompts, such as, *"Show me all the feelings you felt this week about [school, your vacation, your mom being away, your brother, etc.]."*

FEELINGS HIDE-AND-SEEK. Have the child pick three or four feeling pillows and hide them in your office while your eyes are closed. Then hunt for the pillows with the child giving you cues as you move closer ("warm," "warmer," "boiling") or farther away ("cold," "colder," "freezing") from each one. Once a feeling pillow is found, both child and therapist talk about a time they felt that feeling. You can take a turn hiding the pillows too. Again, encourage the child to come up with different situations in which they have felt the feeling rather than letting them repeat the same situations, providing prompts, if necessary. Build on this by having the child talk about a time that someone else they know had that feeling (their dad, siblings, a friend) or by creating a story that incorporates all of the found feelings.

FEELINGS TOSS. Pick multiple feelings from the bowl and create a story using all of them. When each feeling is mentioned in the story, toss that feeling pillow into a chosen target (like a separate basket or empty trash can). Keep score or increase distance from the target to keep the game challenging. The important part of this activity is creating a story together that incorporates the various feelings chosen.

FEELINGS TARGET PRACTICE. Make or purchase a bull's-eye poster that can be attached to a wall or door. Take turns tossing feeling pillows at the target in the middle and talking about each feeling or creating a story about it as it is tossed. In addition, observe yours and the child's feelings as you play. You could say, for example, *"You look like you are feeling **frustrated** because you keep missing the bull's-eye"* or *"I can tell you are feeling something; can you tell me what it is?"* To which the child might respond, *"I'm feeling **sad** that I am losing."* Keep score or increase distance from the target to keep the game challenging. The more you practice talking about feelings with the child, the more comfortable the child will become expressing feelings.

*Note: When you are winning in any of these activities, it can lead to interesting conversations. Children may feel upset and compare themselves negatively to your ability. This opens the door to addressing the value of **practice** and highlighting how much longer and more often you've had the chance to engage in this activity compared to the child. This will help children recognize how and why adults and people older than them have had more experience doing things and therefore have gained more knowledge about those things than the child could possibly have. This recognition will be helpful when kids are teased by older siblings or older kids about something they don't know. Help them develop applicable responses such as, "I'm not as old as you, so I haven't learned that yet" and "You keep winning because you've had more years to practice."*

WALK TO THE FEELING. Invite the child to place the following Kimochis® feeling pillows in different locations in the room: **happy**, **sad**, **mad**, **left out**, **silly**, **frustrated**, **loved**, **scared**, **disappointed**, and **grateful**. Tell the child this is a no-talking game and a way to start becoming more aware of feelings and the ways feelings can help us in life.

Instruct the child to walk to feeling(s) they:

- Enjoyed having this week
- Did not enjoy having this week
- Have a lot of
- Don't have much of
- Want more of
- Want less of
- Want to have every day
- Don't enjoy having but know they have tools for
- Don't enjoy having and want to learn more tools for
- Wish their parents had more of
- Wish their parents had less of
- Know are hard to have (both for themselves and for their friends)
- Think most people want to have more of

Note: These are just suggestions for prompts. You can certainly change them or create your own!

This activity can be expanded by giving the child a choice between two feelings and then giving such prompts as, *"If you had to feel **sad** or **mad**, walk to the feeling you would rather have"* and *"When you lose when playing a game, do you feel more **frustrated** or **sad**?"* This builds awareness of having more than one feeling at a time and helps kids evaluate how they feel about their emotions. The child can also come up with questions and feeling choices for you to answer, which helps them learn that all people experience lots of different feelings. It also allows the child to have some control over session activities and to build trust between the two of you as they see you acknowledging some hard-to-have feelings as well.

WHAT'S ON YOUR PLATE? Here's another great nonverbal activity for times when talking isn't necessary or desirable. Hand the child a paper plate. Toss the Kimochis® feeling pillows on the floor or on a table and have the child turn the feeling pillows word-side-up. Give the child prompts from the list below or of your own making, inviting them to pick up feeling pillows that respond to the prompts and put them on the plate. Alternatively, children can write or draw their feeling word responses on the plate. Sample prompts include:

- *"What feelings do you have at recess?"*
- *"What feelings do you have before going to school?"*
- *"What feelings do you have before bedtime?"*
- *"What feelings do you have when you have to stop doing something you're enjoying?"*
- *"What feelings do you have when someone is unkind to you?"*
- *"What feelings do you have when you see a spider?"*
- *"What feelings do you want to have more of? Less of?"*

For another version of this activity, have the child decorate a plate that stays in your office to be repeatedly used as a check-in. As the child enters each session, prompt them to put the feelings they experienced that week on the plate. You can choose to talk about the pillows they picked or to not talk about them, as it's helpful for children just to acknowledge their feelings and have them known to others. Or you can extend this activity by providing additional prompts, such as:

- *"Pick up your favorite feeling from this week."*
- *"Add two feelings to your plate that you wish you had experienced this week."*
- *"Take off the feeling that was the hardest to have."*
- *"Show me the feeling you felt you had tools for to make things better for yourself."*

Again, the child can guide you in doing this activity as well, as a way of enhancing their awareness that adults also have a wide range of feelings.

FEELINGS STORIES. Ask the child to pick three or four objects in your office. Then have them randomly select three or four feeling pillows from the basket. Have the child create a story using the objects and the feelings. If they need some help or encouragement, you can join in creating the story and adding your own objects and feeling pillows. This activity gives children an opportunity to talk about feelings that aren't specifically about themselves.

Another variation on this activity is to read a story aloud together and have the child pull out the corresponding pillows as they recognize the feelings that different characters in the story are having. If needed, help the child consider what is being felt and pull feelings with them as you read. Or you can even gather the feeling pillows you know will be encountered in the story and instruct the child to pick up each one when they hear it occurring in the story. Wrap up by sharing how you both admired or did not admire how feelings were handled. For example, what did you both think was helpful and what might you do differently if you found yourself in a similar situation?

STORY OF MY DAY. Take turns with the child talking about your day or week as you incorporate the Kimochis® feeling pillows into your discussion. For example, *"When I got up, I felt **sleepy** and **cranky**. Then my dog came in and licked me, so I felt a little **happy**."* Pull the feelings or point to them as they're mentioned.

Note: You can help children along with their stories to lengthen and deepen them with such prompts as: "At breakfast today, I had _____, and that made me feel _____. Then at school, the teacher told us to _____, and I felt _____."

Group 2: Feelings Are Multidimensional

• • • • • • • • • • • • • • • • • •

KIMOCHIS® FEELINGS FACT:
Feelings are more than just words.

This section of the guide focuses on two central tenets about feelings:

1. **Feelings are physical**—they have size and weight. Feelings take up space inside us, affect how we look, act, react, and impact the world we interact with and inhabit. Our bodies often show and can help us know what we are feeling. The more attention we give to what we feel in our bodies, the more we can learn about how we are feeling emotionally. We might have a stomachache before a test, want to kick someone when we're mad, or clench our hands when we're scared.

2. **Feelings fuel behavior**, so being aware of what we feel is important because our emotions often determine how we act. Sometimes people aren't even aware of the feelings that are driving their actions. And sometimes people know what they are feeling, but they're not aware of how that emotion is coming across in their facial expression, word choice, tone of voice, and body language.

It is crucial to distinguish between the feeling being felt and the behavioral way it gets expressed. In other words, the upset feeling itself isn't the problem, but how it's communicated can be problematic. Kids get in trouble for acting out when they feel mad. Consequently, they often come to believe that feeling mad is wrong. Kimochis® instead wants to teach kids: It's okay to be mad, but it's not okay to be mean.

Therapeutic Objective:
Establish the connection between mind and body. Learn that feelings are physical.

Note: As you proceed through these activities, apply your observations about the child to help them build the mind-body connection. Comment on what the child is showing you about the feelings they are having while doing the activities. For example, "You really seem to be enjoying this activity! I can tell because your eyes are wide open and your legs started to bounce." Or, "You are telling me with your words that you're feeling mad, but I'm wondering if you're also feeling sad, because you are sitting hunched over, your mouth is turned downward, your voice is quiet, and you are speaking slowly." Observe the child's reaction but do not challenge it if they disagree with you.

The Activities

WHERE FEELINGS ARE FELT. Take turns with the child picking Kimochis® feeling pillows out of your bowl or basket. Hold each pillow against the place(s) on your body where you might feel that feeling. Demonstrate what your body looks like when having that feeling. This can be a nonverbal activity, or you can both describe where feelings are felt and what you see when the other person shows you what the feeling looks like.

If the child needs help understanding how feelings are physical sensations, prompt them with questions like, *"I wonder if kicking over your friend's building-block tower was your legs' way of letting you know that you were **mad**?" "When you scrunch up your eyes and put your hands in front of your face, is that one way your body is saying you're **scared**?" "What does your body want to do when you feel **excited** … **nervous** … **surprised**?"* To add a little distance or objectivity, these questions can be asked about other people or even fictional characters: *"How does your mommy's body show when she's feeling **loved**?"*

You can build on this exercise by getting a roll of craft paper and rolling it out just past the length of the child's body. Either draw an outline or trace the child's body on the paper. You can write in the feeling words where they identified them earlier, or you can keep the drawing blank and use the pillows instead to respond to prompts to strengthen the mind-body connection.

With all of the feeling pillows within reach, ask the child to answer how they feel in the following scenarios and then place the chosen feeling pillow on the drawing of their body where they sense that feeling. How do they feel when they:

- Take a test
- Get into bed for the night
- Play with their best friend
- Hear their parents argue
- Make a mistake

Tip: Label the drawing with the child's name and keep it rolled up in your office for future sessions when you want to talk about where and how emotions are physically felt.

FEELINGS LEAD TO ACTIONS. Sprinkle the Kimochis® feeling pillows all around the room. Take turns picking up the pillows, saying and showing different ways people might express this feeling. For example, for **suprised**, a person might say, *"Oh my goodness! I never expected that!"* or they might open their mouth wide and jump up and down. For **mad**, a person might stomp their feet, cover their face in a scowl, or put their fists up. Together, decide if you think these actions are helpful or hurtful for each feeling. To keep this activity nonverbal, you can supply the words and behaviors and let the child give a thumbs-up if they think the action is helpful or a thumbs-down if they think the action is not helpful. Explain that this activity shows how feelings can fuel our behavior.

SIZE MATTERS. Feelings come in different sizes, and sizes can change over time. Apart from just having children explain how big a feeling is by using their body to show it, these next three activities (on size, shape, and weight) add volume, texture, and dimension to what is felt.

Begin by having the child pick a feeling they have had recently. This can be a feeling they like to have or a hard-to-have feeling. Now get a balloon and tell the child that you are going to blow it up until they say *"Stop!"* to indicate how big the feeling feels/felt. Afterward, add more air and let some out to show how the size of a feeling can inflate and deflate, can expand and shrink.

Another way to represent the size of an emotion is to use ribbon to show how long the child's feeling is, how far it reaches. Have the child pick a specific situation they're dealing with. Then have them identify the feelings they have about this situation and roll out the ribbon to show how large or long each of those feelings is to them. Cut the ribbons where the child indicates, write the name of each feeling sideways on the corresponding ribbon, then tape the ribbons to a piece of paper so they dangle downward. Label the paper with the situation name (like *Bad Grade at School* or *Being Grounded* or *Argument with Best Friend*). As the child develops tools and creates habits for dealing with this situation, return to the paper and snip some length off each ribbon as the feeling it represents becomes more manageable.

THE SHAPE OF THINGS. For this exercise, gather any useful and applicable craft supplies you can, like paper and colored pencils/crayons/markers, pipe cleaners, Play-Doh, or clay. Have the child pick a feeling and then have them think about what shape that feeling might have. Is it smooth or rough? Sharp or rounded? Tall and skinny or short and squat? Have them draw, mold, or create the shape of the feeling. Express interest and curiosity about what they've created and the colors they've chosen as they explain the shape to you. Repeat this exercise with other feelings.

THE WEIGHT OF IT. It's common to talk about feelings "weighing" on us, usually hard-to-have feelings. Ask the child to pick out some of their hard-to-have feelings and consider how much each of those feelings weighs. Let the child roam your office or therapy space to find items that demonstrate the weight of their feelings—a paperweight, books, a toy, your desk. If nothing in the immediate environment seems to fit the feeling at hand, ask the child to imagine what *would* equal the weight of the feeling—a large dog, a car, a mountain. Alternatively, use a small scale, letting the child place on it something that represents the weight of what they are feeling. Compare the weights of their different hard-to-have feelings.

Conversely, there are some nice-to-have feelings that seem hard to hold on to. These feelings seem almost weightless and just float away. Repeat the process above with a few feelings the child enjoys having. By making these feelings visible and concrete, you'll help kids learn that they can hold on to them.

To expand this exercise, use some kind of see-through container that has a lid (you can bring one in yourself or ask the child to bring one in). Have the child make and attach a label for the container that reads: *Feelings I Like Feeling.* On cardstock rectangles, have the child write down feelings they enjoy feeling and, on the back, examples of when they've felt that way. For example, for **proud**, they might write, *After finishing my presentation to the class* and *When I complete my chores at home.* For **hopeful**, they might write, *I felt hopeful when my mom got a good report from her doctor.* Younger children may also want to draw a picture of what they are feeling.

Put the cards in the container and let the child take the container home with them, supplying extra cards so they can add more feelings they want to hold on to. Decide with them where they should keep the container so that it will be seen and remembered often. When a child is experiencing hard-to-have feelings, they can go to their container and "see" times when they've felt better, assuring themselves that they will feel better again.

Another way to make enjoyable feelings more weighty is to again write them down on a small piece of paper, but then "anchor" each feeling to something significant—like a stone or wooden block—using tape, glue, or Velcro. Or they can even write the feeling directly on flat rocks or blocks with a marker. These, too, can be added to the *Feelings I Like Feeling* container or placed somewhere in their room where they can readily see them for comforting reminders.

WHERE DO YOU STAND? Another way of exploring how our emotions affect us is to show how close to or distant from a feeling we want to be. Ask the child to pick one feeling they enjoy feeling and one they don't enjoy. Put both feeling pillows on the floor. Starting with one of the feelings, ask the child to recall a time they felt that feeling. Ask them to try to re-create that feeling inside them now.

Next, tell the child to stand as near to or as far from the pillow as they want in response to the prompt: *"How much do you enjoy having this feeling?"* Repeat with the other pillow. Practice this with multiple feelings, asking the child to be aware of how each feeling affects them physically. Ask them to show you with their body and face how that feeling makes them feel. Ask what having that feeling makes them want to do (for instance, run away, dance, freeze, curl up, yell).

WHAT FEELINGS DO YOU KNOW *NOW*? As the child's feelings vocabulary grows by working through these sections and doing the activities, take the time to refer back to the feelings poster they created in Group 1 and add new feelings to it. Have them pick the top three feelings they've had this week. You can ask the child to touch or say where that feeling was felt in their body. Ask if there is a thought that goes with that feeling and what having that thought and feeling made them do or made them want to do.

SHOW OFF. Explain to the child that we can create more of the positive feelings we want to have by using our bodies. For example, when we smile, we send our body positive signals that can help fuel positive feelings like **happy** and **hopeful**. Likewise, when we have upset feelings, we can use our body to move through these feelings toward more contentment. When things don't go our way, for instance, we can shrug our shoulders and remind ourselves, *You win some, you lose some. Things might work out better next time.*

Have the child pick out a feeling that makes them feel upset. You or the child can then demonstrate how having this feeling looks on the body. Ask, *"What can you do with your body to make the feeling smaller?"* Give examples if needed: shrug your shoulders, snap your fingers, shake it off, stomp, push against a wall with your arms, legs, or whole body. Practice having different upset feelings and trying different ways to help those feelings feel smaller inside. What works for the child? What doesn't?

Now have the child pick out a feeling they want to have more of, like **hopeful**, **grateful**, or **friendly**. Together, consider how the body can contribute to feeling more of that feeling. For example, take a big, deep breath, clasp your hands together, give yourself a hug, give yourself a pat on the back, smile.

Ask the child to practice using some of these tools at home and to report back next week on what they tried and how it worked or didn't. Keep practicing until the child finds what works for them.

Group 3: Feelings Like Being Felt

KIMOCHIS® FEELINGS FACT:
Feelings don't like to be ignored.

Feelings want to be acknowledged. When we don't judge them, it's easier to do this. People need feelings—and lots of them. Also, people can feel more than one feeling at a time. Not only that, but enjoyable feelings and unenjoyable feelings can be felt at the same time. When feelings make us uncomfortable, it is common to try to not feel them. There are lots of ways to do this. Kids and adults will often go to great lengths to avoid upsetting feelings: ignore them, deny them, hide from them, numb themselves against them, push them away, laugh them off, or bury them deep down. Cutting off feelings in childhood, though, creates grown-ups who are cut off from parts of themselves. People also often have a hard time letting themselves feel positive things about themselves. The Kimochis® Way believes that all people should feel entitled and empowered to feel what they feel and to feel good about themselves. This section is focused on helping the kids you work with learn to acknowledge what they feel and then learn communication tools that will equip them to make themselves feel better.

Therapeutic Objective:
Help children accept that feelings happen and learn to let themselves feel whatever it is they feel in order to name it and choose how to handle it.

The Activities

FEELING "FINE." One of the most common questions people ask is: *"How are you?"* And most often, the reply will be *"Fine"* or *"Good."* And then the conversation just moves on. Rather than just moving on, help the children you work with delve deeper into this question by prompting further: *"Well, if you weren't feeling fine, what would you be feeling?"* or *"Okay, but what else are you feeling?"* Pull out the bowl of Kimochis® feeling pillows and let the child choose other feelings they are experiencing. This activity helps kids get more in touch with themselves and with what is going on internally right at the start of your time together.

ALL BOXED UP. Get a small container with a lid and have the child fill it with all the feelings they wish they didn't have to feel. (The container should be large enough to hold about four feeling pillows but small enough that it cannot be closed with any more feelings in it.) When the lid won't close or it pops back open or feelings spill out of it, observe the child's reaction. Talk to them about what is happening. Explain that this is what happens with feelings when we try not to feel them by stuffing them down. Share instances when this has happened or could happen. This can then lead to a discussion about situations they're dealing with in which their feelings may be "all boxed up."

Go on to explain that when feelings get all boxed up, behavior can be affected, causing us to make mistakes in how we act or what we say. See if the child can talk about mistakes they may have made. Do they know other people who have made mistakes due to their own boxed-up feelings? Together, consider ways to grow from these mistakes and/or make amends.

HOLDINGS HINDRANCE. Ask the child to pick some Kimochis® pillows of feelings they don't enjoy having or feelings they try not to let themselves have. Take two balloons, inflate them, and tie them off. Hand the balloons to the child and tell them that you are going to ask them to do a series of tasks and that they have to hold the balloons while completing the tasks. (In place of balloons, you could use two other objects—something that would be heavy or bulky in their hands). Then proceed through some tasks that become increasingly difficult to do with their hands full, like having them jump up and down, touch the ground, pick up a toy and play with it, scratch their back, unwrap a piece of candy.

Afterward, ask the child what it felt like to try to do something while something else was hindering their ability to do it. Explain that trying to avoid feelings is like this: When there are too many or they are big, the feelings we are holding make it harder to do other things that we need and want to do.

A variation on this activity that also demonstrates the effect of holding in feelings is to again ask the child to pick out some unenjoyable feelings, then sit with their legs out in front of them with those feeling pillows in their lap. Ask them to try to scootch to the other side of the room, to curl up in a ball, to do a somersault. Observe what happens, then ask: *"What's it like to try to move with all those feelings on you? How much effort does it take to keep them all in your lap?"* Invariably, some of the feeling pillows will escape. Use this as a way to show that holding on to too many feelings at once causes them to spill over. Explain that when hard-to-have feelings spill over, they create hard-to-deal-with behaviors, which in turn can cause us to make mistakes in our interactions with others. This creates another opportunity to talk about times this has happened to the child or to someone they know.

FEELING OPPOSITES. Kids are often surprised and sometimes confused to realize that they can have very opposing feelings about a single event. For example, having a new baby sister can make them feel **happy**, **excited**, and **curious**, but it can also make them feel **sad**, **left out**, and **insecure**.

To help kids explore opposing feelings in a visible way, use two paper plates, drawing a smiley face on one and a frowning face on the other. As you give them the following prompts (or any others of your choosing), have the child place all of the enjoyable and unenjoyable feelings that go along with these scenarios on the respective plates:

- Starting the school year
- Ending the school year
- Moving on to a new school after graduation
- Moving to a new neighborhood or out of state
- Birth of a sibling
- Giving up their room when a favorite relative comes to visit
- Having a birthday party
- Going to sleepaway camp in the summer

Note: If the child insists that only one feeling applies to each prompt, pull out other feelings you have had in similar situations or tell them about other children who have had multiple and mixed feelings.

Conclude the activity by assuring kids that ALL of their feelings are acceptable.

ALL AND NOTHING. Tell kids that people often wish they could be happy all the time and feel only good feelings. But the truth is, we all need to experience a whole bunch of feelings because unpleasant things can and do happen, and we need to have feelings to express that. Additionally, hard-to-have feelings make nice-to-have feelings even nicer. For example, because most kids experience challenging feelings throughout any given school year, they're usually very excited and grateful when summer break arrives.

For this exercise, have the child pick Kimochis® feeling pillows that they think they'd like to have all the time. Using those selected feelings, ask the child which of them they'd feel when:

- Receiving their most wanted gift
- Having a favorite person surprise them with a visit
- Getting a high score on a test

Then ask how those same feelings would help when:

- A sibling ruins their art project for school
- They learn they didn't get chosen for the team or school play
- Someone they love is sick

This first part of the exercise shows kids that nice-to-have feelings can help make hard-to-have experiences better. But now have them pull the feelings they'd actually feel in the second set of scenarios. No doubt they'll pick feelings like **mad, frustrated, disappointed**, and **scared**. Assure the child that these are valid and acceptable feelings and the exact same ones most people would feel in the same situations. So we need hard-to-have feelings to deal with hard-to-have experiences. Remind kids that everyone—parents, siblings, friends, teachers—has these kinds of feelings and they're not all enjoyable, but they're all acceptable. It's just as appropriate to feel **cranky** when you have to wake up early as it is to feel **excited** to go on a field trip; it's just as okay to feel **sad** when someone gets hurt as it is to feel **loved** when you get a hug. No one feels something all of the time or none of the time.

STEP INTO FEELINGS TO CREATE CONFIDENCE. When children want or need to do something that is hard to do—like talking to a teacher, telling a friend they've been hurt by them, trying out for a play or a sport, starting at a new school—it can help to "embody" feelings that will help the child be their best self.

Together with the child, pull out the hard-to-have feelings from the Kimochis® feeling pillows bowl that accompany a hard-to-do situation. Next, pull out positive feelings that might support the child in doing the challenging activity, like **hopeful, optimistic**, and **brave**. Have the child recall a time they felt one of these feelings. Ask them to embody the feeling by demonstrating how they would stand, hold their arms and head. Have them show what expression they would have on their face. Ask what they might say to themselves. Then have them practice stepping in and out of that feeling—literally have them jump or step away to leave that feeling, then step back in to embody it again.

Once that feels comfortable for the child, have them practice the hard thing they need to do while they're embodying the positive feeling. Have them keep practicing in your office until it feels doable, though this may take lots of encouragement and repetition.

As a next step, walk the child through multiple trial runs using this new tool before they apply it in real life by having them create a story about themselves that incorporates the challenging situation and "stepping into" their confidence. Remind them to take their time and to step into their helpful feeling before addressing the hard-to-do thing. This can become a helpful habit to use in any hard-to-handle situation.

Now you're ready to literally create **confidence**. Take a blank Kimochis® feeling pillow or create one using the **Make Your Own Kimochis® Feelings Template** (Appendix E at the back of this guide; see p. 10 for how to use this template). Have the child draw a confident Kimochis® face on one side and write CONFIDENT on the other. Repeat the above exercise with confidence!

When it comes to hard-to-do things, we've found that when this issue involves talking to someone else, it's complicated by that fact that assumptions are made about how the conversation will go. Very often, kids (and adults) assume that a hard-to-have conversation will turn out badly. They assume the teacher will get mad at their question, their friend won't listen to them, or they won't achieve what they want. So ask the kids you work with about their assumptions. Then create stories with them that have different outcomes. Role-play various ways the situation might go. Does imagining a positive outcome change how the child feels about approaching the situation? Does role-playing help the child gain comfort with addressing the situation overall and feeling more confident in handling whichever responses they may encounter? Discussing all of this before the child puts this new tool into practice will pave the way for more likely success!

MAD MASK. Feeling mad is a very common and human emotion, especially for kids, who are just developing their emotional intelligence. Here's some of what we know about mad feelings.

- **Mad** can be a BIG, hard feeling.
- It's often easier to feel **mad** than to feel **sad, hurt, disappointed, left out, sorry.**
- Feeling **mad** is often a gatekeeper to other feelings that we don't want to feel.
- Feeling **mad** can be used as a mask to cover up other feelings we don't enjoy feeling.

Begin by sharing the above points with the child. Then have the child pull the **mad** feeling pillow from your basket or bowl. Ask them to show you their mad face, their mad body. Ask them to use their mad voice. Explain that people can go through life not really realizing that anger is very often just the emotion on the surface of something deeper, so it's worth examining this feeling closely.

Next, pick feelings from the basket that anger can cover up. Place those feeling pillows under something or hide them around the room. (If you're feeling creative, you could devise some kind of gate to put them behind or procure an angry-looking face mask to place on top of them.)

Invite the child to find or uncover the hidden feelings. Once those pillows are revealed or found, consider them one at a time with the child: *"Do you think this is a feeling that could be hiding behind mad?" "Is this something you or someone else might be feeling along with feeling mad?"* To keep it nonverbal, let the child use a thumbs-up or a thumbs-down to let you know if they agree.

To further explore this idea of using anger as a cover-up for other hard-to-have feelings, ask the child to give an example of someone they know who seemed mad but was likely feeling something else underneath, or have them create a story featuring "Mad Mask."

If you wish, you can continue this conversation about anger by posing additional questions—such as, *"When feeling mad, which habits are helpful and which are hurtful?"* and *"What mistakes can people make when they feel mad, and how might they recover?"*—or by role-playing how to correct a mistake. For instance, yell out angrily, *"I hate you!"* But then compose yourself quickly and say, *"I'm sorry I said I hate you when I don't. I'm just feeling really, really mad."*

FEELING PROUD. Pride can sometimes be tough for kids to let themselves experience, because negative judgement often accompanies it. Examples: *"Winning that award wasn't such a big deal." "Everyone else can already ride a bike." "I don't want to sound like I'm bragging."* So talk with the child about times when feeling **proud** is completely warranted. This will not only give them permission to be proud of themselves for accomplishments, but it can open up an important discussion about how we don't judge feelings, we just have them.

Holding the **proud** feeling pillow, have the child describe what they see and think when looking at it. You can repeat the **Where Do You Stand?** activity (on p. 19), or you can ask them to list some things they think they could feel proud of or things others have told them they should be proud of. On a blank sticker, draw the Kimochis® proud face and write PROUD on it. Put the sticker on the child and see if it sticks or if they feel the need to remove it. If it's hard for the child to embrace self-pride, help them build up a tolerance for it over time by substituting other words that are more comfortable for them, like "good," "pleased," "satisfied," and "okay."

BRAVE LEADS THE WAY. Managing hard-to-have feelings is never easy. So we use bravery to guide children through them. As you did in the **Step into Feelings** activity (see p. 24), ask the child to "put on their brave" or "step into their brave" by assuming the physical stance, facial expression, and tone of voice they associate with being **brave** or with doing something that is hard for them to do (like when they learned to ride a bike or had to read out loud in class).

Observe and let them notice and feel the difference between their courageous stance and their normal stance. Are they standing taller? Projecting outward? Eyes open wider? Have the child practice moving in and out of feeling brave.

Next, ask the child to pick out a feeling or two they are struggling with. Perhaps they are **uncomfortable** and **scared** to tell a friend that they've been feeling left out lately. Pass the **brave** feeling pillow to the child to position in front of the other two. Then ask them to role-play with you, practicing what they might say to their friend. Give positive feedback when they use the

Kimochis® Keys to Communication (see p. 6), like making eye contact and using a friendly tone of voice. If the child would like, make a cutout **brave** feeling pillow they can take home with them, keeping it in a pocket so they can touch base with their bravery whenever they need to in real life. Say the words *"Put your brave in front"*—it's a powerful tool to remind children to communicate and act with courage in the face of challenging emotions.

*Note: As mentioned before, you can make take-home copies of ANY of the feelings you want to focus on with the children you work with (use Appendix E: **Make Your Own Kimochis® Feelings Template**), so they can keep them with them at all times to remind them of the tools they're learning. We call this our **Pocketful of Practice**!*

SORRY CAN BE HARD TO SAY. Even when people know they've done something wrong, it can feel nearly impossible to simply say, *"I'm sorry."* Holding the Kimochis® **sorry** feeling pillow in your hand, talk about the word and how it is used. Ask the child how often they think *"I'm sorry"* is said sincerely versus how often it's said because the apologizer is made to say it. Have the child pick out the feelings they have when someone says *"I'm sorry"* to them but doesn't seem to mean it. Then have them pick feelings that show how they feel when someone meaningfully says *"I'm sorry"* to them.

Move on to discussing what it's like to be the one to apologize. Feeling sorry can be confusing for anyone because sometimes when we're told to say it or feel it, we don't mean it, and yet when we truly are sorry about something we've done, it can very hard to admit it.

Pull feelings out of the basket that can make saying sorry so hard, such as **scared** (*"I might get in trouble"*), **disappointed** (*"I know my mom and dad won't like that I did that"*), and **sad** (*"I'm unhappy that I did the wrong thing"*). Put them behind the **sorry** pillow.

Now pick up the **brave** feeling pillow and place it in front of all the others. Remind the child how we can use bravery when we have to communicate something difficult. Feeling brave can help us say *"I'm sorry"* even when we're feeling **scared** or **guilty** or **embarrassed**.

Share with the child that a meaningful apology always includes:

- Making eye contact
- Saying the person's name
- Using a sincere voice and facial expression
- Specifying exactly what you did
- Explaining why you think it was hurtful

Then model a sample sincere apology, such as: *"Delrena, I'm sorry I talked behind your back. That was mean."* Take turns practicing sincere apologies for different scenarios you and the child create until they consistently incorporate the above elements.

Once you see that the child is able to make a sincere apology, it's important to let them know the hard, sad news that sometimes people will not accept their apology. So role-play again—this time having the child meaningfully apologize but not accepting it from your side, the way kids their own age might refuse. Tell them that when this happens, it's best to repeat the apology, slowly and just as sincerely as the first time. Model this for them by repeating their own apology several times, explaining that what tends to happen is that others eventually accept an apology when they can tell that you understand that you hurt them. Debrief the child by describing exactly you did with your face, your voice, and your words that made the other person believe you and then accept your apology.

Finally, reverse the roles again, so that the child learns how to slowly and sincerely repeat their apology with the appropriate accompanying body language. This may take lots and lots of practice, but assure the child that they have the power to remain sincerely sorry even when others are not yet ready to accept their apology and that no one can take their sorry away.

FEELINGS SOUP. Kimochis® soups are a staple in our therapeutic approach because they can be used in multiple ways, like celebrating such special events as birthdays, winter break, and personal accomplishments or working through difficult experiences by breaking them down into separate "ingredients" that feel more manageable, one hard-to-have feeling at a time. So for this activity, get out your mixing spoon and either a large mixing bowl or a soup pot so you can start cooking!

Begin by sprinkling all the Kimochis® feeling pillows on a table or the floor word-side-up. Place the bowl or pot in the middle of them, then invite the child to engage: "Let's make Kimochis® soup!" Start with one that will contain mostly good feelings, like "Vacation Soup." Have them toss in all the feelings they have about taking a vacation.

Note: When it comes to soups containing mostly challenging feelings, like "Getting a Bad Grade Soup," it can be helpful to keep this activity more objective in the beginning by using conditional and third-person language, such as, "What feelings might kids your age have when they get a bad grade?" Once the child gets the hang of making Kimochis® soup, you can make this activity more personal.

Here are some suggested soups for school-age children:

- First Day of School Soup
- Test Soup
- Fighting Soup
- I Am Moving Soup
- Family Soup
- Homework Soup
- Birthday Party Soup
- Recess Soup
- I Want More Soup (feelings the child wants more of)
- Soup I Don't Like (feelings the child wants less of)
- I Need Help Soup (feelings the child wants to work on)

Once a topic or theme is chosen, let the child select any and all feelings they have about that topic and toss the pillows in the pot. You can toss some in too, to make the soup richer and more complex for discussion. Hand them a mixing spoon and let them stir the soup as they explain why they included each "ingredient." For example, *"When I didn't do well on my math test, I felt **embarrassed**. And I also felt **sensitive**, because I didn't want the other kids to think I wasn't as smart as them."* Acknowledge what they've shared with you—*"Yes, that makes sense; I think most people feel embarrassed when they don't do well on an exam"*—and then share your reasons for adding your own ingredients: *"But I'm **curious** about why you got a bad grade. Do you think it was because you didn't study enough or maybe because you didn't understand the directions?"* Then add, *"School is a place for learning. So I'm **hopeful** that your teacher will help you with your math skills and that you'll do better next time."*

Take turns with the child exchanging tips and tricks for managing each feeling. Wrap up this activity by having the child identify one new idea or lesson they learned from this "recipe" that might help them with these particular feelings in the future.

The best thing about this activity is that you can do it over and over—creating new and different soups—talking about how life is a great big bowl of mixed feelings too and learning something new each time. Consider adding a "Soup of the Week" to start off each session, letting the child toss in and mix up all the feelings they had since they last saw you. Once the soup is made, have the child pull out each feeling and discuss which other feelings might have made the situation better. It's a great ice-breaker with unlimited variety and potential!

FEELINGS HELP FEELINGS. Put the **optimistic**, **hopeful**, **loved**, **happy**, **excited**, **grateful**, and **proud** feeling pillows between you and the child. Take turns picking up each feeling and describing what this feeling word means and how it feels inside one's body. For example, **optimistic** makes you feel like things are possible; it's a good feeling in your brain and it fills your heart with hope. Ask the child to pick up one of the positive feelings you have talked about. Explain that you are going to show how positive feelings can help with hard-to-have feelings. Have the child pull a feeling that has been hard to have this week. Put the positive feeling on top or under the hard-to-have feeling and then start a discussion about how this positive feeling can support, comfort, and help the child with the hard-to-have feeling. For example, **loved** can help someone remember that they are loved by many others while they're going through sadness and grief over the loss of a beloved relative or pet.

MORE AND LESS. It is important for kids to know that other people can help them with their feelings, but it's just as important that they know that they can develop **tools** and **habits** to help themselves feel better when going through tough times.

For this activity, both you and the child choose one Kimochis® feeling you are currently enjoying. Talk about ways you can continue to have this feeling in the coming week. Explain that feelings don't just happen to us, we can make them happen for ourselves, then brainstorm about ways to bring more of this feeling into each of your lives. For example, you can increase feeling **grateful** by making a list of all the things you are thankful to have in your life.

Repeat the exercise with a feeling each of you didn't enjoy having this week. Now brainstorm about ways to have less of this feeling in the coming week. For example, to make **mad** smaller, you can count to 10 in your head before reacting, you can go to a quiet place for a few minutes to get calm, you can practice deep breathing.

Lastly, each of you pulls feelings you will have if you can manage to make more or less of your chosen feelings.

Note: This is a great activity to end your sessions because it sets an intention for the coming week. Take a photo with your phone of the feelings the child chose to work on, then begin the next session with a meaningful conversation about how much progress they made, how their set goals played out.

FEELINGS FUEL BEHAVIOR. Once children begin to embody their feelings and experience them in concrete ways, they can learn to develop **positive communication tools** to help their feelings get bigger or smaller. These tools also help children develop more effective ways of dealing with communication mistakes.

Begin by printing out the **Kimochis® Feelings Fuel Behavior Worksheet** (see Appendix F at the back of this guide). Then remind the child what they learned in the **Size Matters** activity above (see p. 18)—that feelings come in different sizes—and tell them that there are things they can do to make feelings bigger or smaller, to make hard-to-have feelings easier to manage and nice-to-have feelings easier to hold on to. Have the child choose one Kimochis® feeling pillow that they'd like to work with to start. Write the name of the feeling in the first row of the worksheet. Is this a feeling the child wants to make **bigger** or **smaller**? Check whichever box they choose. Ask how they'd like to approach dealing with this feeling. Would they like to **think**, **do**, or **share** something about the feeling? Put a check in the column they choose. Then brainstorm* with them about ways to deal with that feeling. Whatever way you come up with becomes the **tool** that will be written in that section of the feelings chart. With practice, a tool becomes a habit.

Any feeling can be approached in multiple ways. For example, entries on the feelings worksheet might look like this:

Mad/Smaller/Think: *Mad makes me feel bad, and I want to have fun playing with my friend.*

Mad/Smaller/Do: *Punch a pillow and scream into it until I feel less mad.*

Mad/Bigger/Share: *Say to my sister, "I don't like you coming into my room without knocking. Please knock next time."*

Note: Sometimes feelings need to get bigger before we're ready to address them.

In our experience, brainstorming is a tool worth developing that deserves the practice it takes to make it a habit. People often get tripped up on brainstorming because they judge their ideas before even getting them out of their head. We promote jotting down EVERY idea that comes to mind, regardless of how wild or wacky it may seem at first. The brain works in mysterious ways, and we don't know which seemingly dumb idea might spark another, better idea. After jotting down every idea, go back and examine them more closely. Some ideas may be good but not doable. Others may be easy to do but not effective. So go through them one at a time and evaluate them individually. Organize them into themes. Flesh them out. Create a plan. Execute the plan. Brainstorming can be a detailed process and it may take a few sessions to figure out how you want to deal with the situation/feeling, but it's worth the time and effort when you hit upon a suitable solution!

PILLOW FIGHT. This is mostly just a game for fun, but fun always has a therapeutic benefit! It demonstrates that all feelings can be handled and managed. Feelings can create a big mess, but with tools, resiliency, and maybe some help from others, they can always be tidied up.

Tell the child that you are going to have a Kimochis® pillow fight. Pick one theme to start, like feelings you enjoy having, then toss those pillows at each other one at a time. (Make a rule that pillows are not to be thrown at faces or at anything important in your therapy room.) Proceed through a couple other themes, letting the pillow fight be organic and spontaneous, with laughter and no scripted language.

When you're done, ask the child to help gather all the pillows and return them to where they belong. As you jointly attend to this task, ask the child: *"Why do you think people fight?" "What do fights look like at school?" "At home?" "What is not helpful about fighting?"* Talk about how feelings can be messy but manageable.

A Kimochis® pillow fight can be a very effective conversation starter, but, really, talking isn't as important here as just sharing fun and laughter in this safe space between you and the child. Once you've introduced them to this activity, kids might request a pillow fight at other times—maybe as a way to let off some steam without using hurtful words or actions when they have upset feelings—and you can incorporate it into your sessions when suitable to relieve tension, maybe to lighten a heavy moment or as a way to bring up a topic they're reluctant to broach. You can just toss a strategically chosen pillow at them and say, *"How about this one?"* Let the child respond and toss it back at you.

As for young kids, we've learned from experience that they enjoy having all the pillows dumped on them at once and rolling around in them. This shows them just how many feelings they have inside and that they have what it takes to handle all of them!

Group 4: Feelings Are for Sharing

KIMOCHIS® FEELINGS FACT:
Some feelings can be hard to have and hard to share.

Some feelings we want to have and others we don't. Sometimes other people don't want us to have the feelings we are experiencing. Very often, kids develop beliefs about certain feelings being okay and others being unacceptable: *"I can't talk about winning the spelling contest—that's bragging." "When I told my brother about my friend being mean to me, he said, 'Ignore him.'" "Feeling scared or showing sadness means you're weak."* Learning to express feelings verbally prevents people from developing hurtful habits as ways of expressing themselves. Screaming, saying mean words, or physically lashing out when you feel mad ends up with people getting in trouble. This leads to the belief that it is not okay to feel mad.

We want to help children learn that ALL feelings are acceptable. We don't judge feelings as good or bad, right or wrong, okay or not okay to have. It isn't what you feel but how you experience it—and then, when, with whom, and how you share your feelings—that can impact these beliefs.

Therapeutic Objective:
Help children learn to evaluate who they can share their feelings with and when sharing feelings can help them feel better.

The Activities

FEELING SAFELY. Ask the child to sort all the Kimochis® feeling pillows into three different piles: (1) feelings they are comfortable sharing; (2) feelings they keep to themselves; and (3) feelings they wish they could share but don't. Listen to and observe how they make their decisions when sorting.

Start a conversation about trust. Create a list with the child of the qualities they want in someone to share feelings with and to help them with their problems. Who will listen? Who will help?

Note: You may need to explain that sometimes people hold their feelings in until they find a person to confide in, a person they trust to listen and help them. Encourage the child to keep looking until they find a few people like that. Hopefully, you'll be one of them!

On squares of paper, have the child write down or tell you the names of important people in their life: Mom, Dad, siblings, relatives, other adults, friends, pets. Write one name on each piece of paper. Now ask the child to sort these into three different piles too: (1) people they can share their feelings with; (2) people they don't or can't share their feelings with; and (3) people they wish they could share their feelings with but don't.

Combine the feeling pillows and the people cards that align (that is, put the the pile of feelings they are comfortable sharing with the people they freely share feelings with, etc.). Ask them if the feeling words on the pillows match up with the people. This part of the activity may lead to greater differentiation among the pillows and the people, and that's a good thing, as it illustrates the child's awareness that they seek out different people for sharing different types of feelings. For example, Uncle Steve may be perfect to talk to when feeling sad, but sister Jenny is the best person to go to when feeling mad, and Mom is best when feeling silly. Tell the child that knowing who they can go to with different kinds of feelings is an important tool.

A variation on this activity is to just make and then spread out the name cards. Then pull a variety of feelings one at a time and let the child decide who might be good for helping with that particular feeling. For instance, *"I think Grandpa could help me with **frustrated**, because even when I see him irritated, his voice stays calm."*

DARE TO SHARE. People often don't share one feeling because other feelings make it hard for them to do so. For example, a child who is feeling upset about being teased may feel **shy** and/or **scared** about saying anything because of how peers may react.

Ask the child to select feelings that might be hard for kids their age to share. Then ask them to choose other feelings that could make it hard to share the original feeling. If they choose **mad**, for instance, that may be hard to share because **scared** or **embarrassed** accompanies it. Acknowledge that it makes sense to feel scared and/or embarrassed to share mad feelings. Think out loud with the child about what they know or have seen that could help them deal with and share their upset feelings.

You will want to repeat this exercise making it more personal to the child's feelings.

FEELINGS SANDWICH. This activity is intended to help kids recognize that even hard-to-have feelings can be digested when "sandwiched" between feelings with a preferred flavor. It also helps kids realize that even when they are feeling upset, they have access to other feelings that can help them feel better.

To start, pull a feeling pillow that is hard for you to have and show it to the child. Next, pull two positive feelings that make the difficult one easier for you to manage and put one on top and one on bottom of the hard-to-have feeling to create a Kimochis® sandwich. Explain to the child how these two positive feelings give you comfort and support when you need it. For example: *"I was **disappointed** last week when a paper I wrote didn't get accepted for publication. But then I thought about how **proud** I am of the work I do for people, and I'm **hopeful** that I can share more of that work in a different publication, maybe, or in the next paper I write."* Tell the child that they, too, can make a Kimochis® sandwich to help themselves feel better when they are having a difficult time, and then invite them to do so.

Walk them through the steps above one at time: have them pull a hard-to-have feeling and share with you why they're feeling it. Then ask the child to pull two other feelings that make them feel good. Ask them to consider how those two enjoyable feelings can make the hard-to-have feeling better.

Another example: The child comes to therapy to manage feelings about the loss of a grandparent. If **sad** is chosen as the hard-to-have feeling in the middle, then they could place **grateful** on top (for having such a wonderful grandparent as long as they did) and **loved** on the bottom (knowing how much their grandparent adored them and that their parents care about helping them through the loss). This can make it much easier to cope with the sadness of mourning.

Extend this activity by having the child consider if there are other sandwiches they can make with this same hard-to-have feeling that would make it easier to swallow. Talk about, draw pictures, or write down things the child can do to help themselves feel surrounded and protected by the better feelings when the hard feelings arise.

MORE SANDWICHES. The sandwich approach can be used in multiple ways—for hard-to-share feelings, not just hard-to-have feelings. Letting other people know what we're feeling is essential, but it can be quite difficult and it takes practice.

With the child, pick out a hard-to-share feeling. Then pull out **brave** and put it under the hard-to-share feeling, telling the child that it takes courage to open up, but assuring them that things usually work out well when they do. Have them practice sharing the difficult feeling with a prompt like, *"It makes me feel _____ when you _____"* or *"I feel _____ for doing_____."* Now top the sandwich with **proud**, acknowledging the child for sharing the challenging feeling. Ask the child to share any feelings of accomplishment they may have for doing this activity. Repeat this cycle with any other difficult-to-share feelings you are working on with the child. Ask the child if they'd like to try sharing feelings with someone before your next meeting. Be sure to follow up when they come back to see how it went.

Note: It is important to distinguish for children the difference between saying what they think/feel/want/need to say and having the other person react in the way they want them to or think they should. Mom may still say "no" to something they ask and a friend may still be mean, but speaking up for oneself builds confidence and inner strength.

UNDER AND OVER. Have the child pour all the Kimochis® feeling pillows out of the basket. Turn the basket upside down. Telling them you will close your eyes so you can't watch, instruct the child to put under the basket feelings they think kids their age would prefer not sharing. Next, ask the child to place on top of the basket feelings they think kids their age are more comfortable sharing.

When you open your eyes, make some guesses as to which feelings might be under the basket and let the child count how many you get right. Together, make some guesses as to why people might not want to share their "under-the-basket" feelings. For instance, if someone feels **shy**, others might tease them. Then have the child take each feeling that's hidden under the basket and make a list of things that would make it easier to share these feelings with others. Reassure the child that everyone needs just one safe person to share all their feelings with.

Ask the child if they have a person in their life who does or says things that lets them know it's safe to share with them. Encourage the child to talk to this person about their feelings. Ask them what makes it easier to speak to this person about their feelings. What does this person do or not do that helps the child share with them? Just being aware of who they can confide in may lead them to do so more frequently.

Continue the conversation and get curious with the child about qualities they have that encourage people to want to share their under-the-basket feelings with them. End this activity by assuring the child that you are someone they can trust their hidden feelings to.

COVER UP. When people are having hard-to-have feelings that they're not ready to share, they often "cover them up." At school, kids might show one feeling on the outside (looking happy or confident when joining a new group) that is quite different from what they're actually feeling on the inside (like lonely or insecure). Or when things are tough at home: on the outside, kids act with their friends like everything is just fine, but on the inside, they're feeling sad and confused.

Note: Make sure to explain to the child that it can sometimes be very useful to cover up—when we need to concentrate on schoolwork, for example, or when there's not someone nearby we can share our feelings with or when we'd rather have fun with our friends than dwell on something that is bothering us.

Ask the child to think about a time they had feelings they didn't want to share or something they are working on with you that is hard to talk about. If they don't want to identify the situation they're struggling with, that's okay. They can still pick feelings and sort them into two piles of those they are "keeping inside" and those they are "showing on the outside." These can also be talked about as "private" and "public" feelings.

Talk with the child about why they sometimes cover up. Do they think other people do this too? Often, kids think that they're the only ones who feel a certain way about what they're dealing with, so it's helpful for them to learn that other people sometimes keep their feelings on the inside as well.

Note: This exercise can lead to a discussion about the feelings-behavior link. What does the child believe happens when big, heavy, hard-to-have feelings are kept inside for too long? Is it possible that their friend who's been less friendly lately or their dad who's been snapping more often lately might be doing some "covering up" of their own?

FEELINGS HUNT. To both expand on the theme of inside/outside feelings and extend the hide-and-seek activity from Group 1, invite the child to hide some Kimochis® feeling pillows around the room—those feelings that they think people do not like to feel or share. Once they're all hidden, you hunt for them.

As you find each one, invite the child to pull feelings from the basket that make the hidden feeling hard to have or hard to share. For **sad**, for example, maybe it's hidden inside when someone feels **embarrassed**, **scared**, or **insecure**. Then ask the child to pick out a feeling that could make it easier to share this hard-to-have feeling.

Now it's your turn to hide some hard-to-have feelings you believe the child is currently struggling with. When the child finds each feeling, have them give you a thumbs-up or a thumbs-down as to whether or not they're experiencing it.

Note: Depending on how established the relationship is between you and the child, you can accept their response or you can gently challenge it to encourage more openness about acknowledging and sharing the hard-to-have feeling.

OTHER PEOPLE'S SHOES. This activity helps kids learn about feelings other people have and that those feelings may be the same as or different from theirs. Begin by helping children understand the concept of *perspective taking.* Select an object in your therapy space, like a patterned pillow, large toy, or picture on your wall. Take turns saying what you each see. As the therapist, you want to point out different things than what the child sees. Acknowledge what the child sees and help them see what you observe. After three or four observations, ask the child, *"Are the things you see correct?"* Follow up with, *"Are the things I see correct?"* (The answer to both questions should be "yes.") Ask, *"Can we look at the same thing but see it differently?"* Explain that this is what often happens in disagreements: People see different things in what happened, and both can be right.

Note: This activity is most effective when repeated, as perspective taking can take some time to learn.

Next, have a large pair of shoes available that the child can step into or draw a large pair of shoes on a piece of paper that the child can stand on. Reinforce that people can feel differently about the same situation. Give the following example: *"You are playfully teasing someone, and you think it's funny."* Have the child pick out the feelings they would have in this situation (like **silly**, **friendly**). Then have the child step into the pair of shoes and think about what the other person could be feeling. Pick those feelings out of the basket. Compare the two sets of feelings. Ask about other times when the child felt differently from someone else or vice versa. *"How do you act depending on how you feel?"* *"How easy or hard is it to wear another person's shoes, see things from their perspective?"*

CURIOUS CAT. Pull out the **curious** feeling pillow and share that curiosity can be a very powerful tool in life because it helps us understand why we do some of the things we do. Curiosity can help us have more compassion for self and others. Ask the child:

- *"What does 'curiosity' mean?"*
- *"How can curiosity be helpful?"*
- *"When is curiosity not helpful?"*
- *"Can curiosity get you into trouble?"*

Ask the child to think of a time when someone did something they didn't understand (or create a situation for the child to consider). Ask the child to be curious by considering reasons why the person may have behaved as they did. (If the child makes it general or personal—*"They were just being mean"* or *"She wanted to make me cry"*—ask them to step into the other person's shoes and consider what that person may have been experiencing or going through that caused them to act that way.) For example, if they're bothered by someone who frequently interrupts them when they speak, ask them to be curious about what causes this person to interrupt.

Note: We forget that others regularly behave on the basis of their own internal situations, and while their behavior may impact us, it is not really about us. Understanding this can help kids learn to react with compassion rather than taking things personally and responding in anger.

Take out the **kind** Kimochis® feeling pillow. Ask the child how they would want others to treat them when they aren't being quite themselves. Then ask what they can do if someone they care about is behaving differently than they usually do.

As the child holds the **curious** feeling, ask them to consider some of their own behaviors. Say, *"Let's practice being curious,"* and then follow it up with a pertinent example they've shared with you. For example, *"Why did you [knock down the blocks your sister was playing with or hide your mother's purse]? Understanding the impulse or motivation behind your own behavior can help you behave differently the next time you might want to act in a way that isn't helpful to you or those around you."*

WHAT'S ON YOUR PLATE: PART 2. In Group 1, this activity applied to children learning about their own feelings. Here, the activity is expanded by having children consider the feelings of others as well.

Give the child a paper plate. Toss all the Kimochis® pillows on the floor or a table and have the child turn them word-side-up without talking. Give the child a prompt and invite them to pick up various feeling pillows in response to the prompts. Children can alternatively draw or write feeling words on their plate.

- *"What feelings do you think one of the popular kids has at recess?"*
- *"What feelings do you think your mom or dad has before going to work?"*
- *"What feelings do you think your friend has before bedtime?"*
- *"What feelings do you think your brother has when he has to stop doing something he's enjoying?"*
- *"What feelings do you think your cousin has when someone is unkind to her?"*
- *"What feelings do you think your sister has about playing basketball?"*
- *"What feelings do you think your mom has about going to the beach?"*
- *"What feelings do you think your grandma has about math?"*

After the child chooses the feelings for each prompt, ask them if they would feel the same feelings or different ones. Talk about how people can have different reactions to the same situation.

COMPASSION STEW. Ask the child about someone they know who may be having or has had hard-to-have feelings, then have them put all those feeling pillows in a stew pot. Ask the child how they can tell that the other person is upset: What do they see, feel, and hear that lets them know what the person may be experiencing? Talk about what might be causing the other person's feelings. Together, generate possible reasons the other person is upset.

Note: Kids (and adults) often make assumptions about what is going on without knowing all the facts. It may be clear that a friend is sad because their cat died, but there could be several reasons why a friend is off sulking in the corner.

Next, have the child pull feelings that they have in response to the other person's upset (including any that may already be in the pot) and add those feelings to the stew. Then add feelings the child believes could help that person feel better.

As the child stirs the pot of feelings, talk about compassion—the concern we feel for someone else who is going through a hard time. Brainstorm with the child about things they could do or say to help the person have more of the better feelings. Ask what they might want someone else to do for them if they were in that situation. Role-play situations in which one of you is hurting and the other is helping. Practice simple statements, such as, *"Sam, it looks like you are feeling _____. I'm sorry you're feeling this way. Can I help? Do you want to talk?"* Practice giving a gentle pat on the back, arm, or hand.

Explain to the child that the person might not readily admit their own feelings or accept the offer of help, but they will know that they have a true friend who cares enough about them to notice and say something. End by having the child identify which feelings result from offering to help the other person. Mix those into the stew as you talk about how we can all help each other make hard-to-have feelings better.

Note: Children can also make a stew of their own feelings, as learning to be compassionate toward themselves is another tool that will benefit them for life.

HARD TO HEAR BUT GOOD TO KNOW. Other people sometimes get upset with us. That can be hard to hear, but it's good to know because it gives us the chance to try to fix things. In fact, it's actually much harder to deal with people who are upset with us but won't tell us why or won't talk about what happened, right? So explain these ideas to the child, emphasizing that something good can come out of something hard.

Have the child recall a "hard to hear but good to know" experience they had. Then have the child pull out the feelings the other person was having. Next, have them pull the feelings they had in response to knowing the other person was upset with them. (If the child has difficulty thinking of their own "hard to hear but good to know" experience, they can use someone they know as an example instead.)

Get two paper plates and label one *Good Choice Response* and the other *Not Great Response.* Write down samples of each, explaining that "not great responses" are often our first impulse, like yelling, stomping, denying the hard news we've been told, or accusing the other person of something instead. "Good choice responses," in contrast, come about when we give ourselves an opportunity to take a deep breath, think about what we just heard for a minute, and then respond when we're ready. Talk with the child about the potential outcomes for each type of response. For example, *"Say your sister comes into the playroom and screams at you, 'You're such a slob! Why is it always so messy in here?' What would happen if you just yelled back, 'You're the slob! Now get out of here and leave me alone'? ... What would happen if you took a breath, took a minute to look around the room, then calmly answered, 'Maybe you have a point. I'll make sure I put my things away later when I'm done with them'?"*

Ask the child to pull feelings from the Kimochis® basket that describe how they feel about themselves after responding with a not great response versus a good choice response. Role-play a few situations with them that include different types of responses. Talk about the various ways people can work through a problem, including the "agree to disagree" approach. Share with the child ways that people "make up" after resolving a "hard-to-hear" situation, such as a handshake, a hug, making a funny face.

End by letting the child know that we can't control how other people will respond to us. However, we can control how we respond to others and how we can try to repair hurt feelings when they happen. When we do that, we can feel proud of ourselves. Hand the child the **proud** feeling.

Appendix: Kimochis® Resources

This guidebook, where relevant, refers to multiple printouts and tools that you can use to enhance your Kimochis® experience, not just with the activities in this guide, but across the whole Kimochis® curriculum. Make copies of the following handouts and use them often with and for the families you serve.

- Appendix A: Kimochis® 7 Extremely Helpful Ways to Talk About Feelings
- Appendix B: Kimochis® 5 Keys to Communication
- Appendix C: Kimochis® 7 Keys to Communication
- Appendix D: Kimochis® Social-Emotional Learning (SEL) Vocabulary
- Appendix E: Make Your Own Kimochis® Feelings Template
- Appendix F: Kimochis® Feelings Fuel Behavior Worksheet

Kimochis®

7 Extremely Helpful Ways to Talk About Feelings

1 PRACTICE
Practice does not make perfect, but it does make things better and easier. Kimochis® is all about making things better over time. So you will want to repeat these activities over and over in order to provide lots of opportunities to practice and incorporate what's being learned. Say the word "practice" frequently as you direct and repeat activities. Explain that everyone needs to practice in order to learn new things and that practice involves putting in effort and trying again and again. Ultimately, practice is habit-forming.

2 HABIT
 The Kimochis® Way speaks of developing *habits* rather than *skills*. The word "skill" can give the impression that someone either has an ability or does not have that ability. It can also make one think that there is a right and a wrong way to do something. In contrast, consider the word "habit." A habit is often acquired without being directly taught. People can develop not-so-good habits, but with teaching, repetition, practice, positive feedback, coaching, and gentle reminders, people can also learn and form new, positive habits. Using the word "habit" in relation to developing positive communication tools can help kids feel more hopeful that they can learn and improve. It can also encourage children to be more open to redoing or trying again when they forget to use positive communication habits.

3 TOOLS
Talk with the children you're working with about how tools help people. For example, hammers help us build. Pencils help us draw and write. Likewise, communication tools help us make and keep friends, resolve conflict, and do our best in school, at home, and in life. Using the word "tools" during your sessions makes communication sound and feel more tangible and lets children know there are positive actions they can take to express feelings.

4 SIZE
From the very beginning of any conversation about feelings, you can help children make the connection between mind and body by asking them to use their body to show how large their feelings feel. Ask kids to use their arms and hands, feet and legs, to respond to, for example, *"Are you a little mad, medium-sized mad, or really, really big mad?"* Conversely, you might ask, *"Are you feeling a little optimistic, medium-sized optimistic, or really, really big optimistic?"* The Kimochis® activities will focus on this directly in order to help children understand that feelings can be felt in different intensities, can come and go, and can be made more manageable by learning things to say and do to help them feel better. It's important to convey that feelings can be made smaller and bigger depending on whether we want to feel more or less of them.

Kimochis®

7 Extremely Helpful Ways to Talk About Feelings

5 **STORY**
Most people start a conversation with the standard "wh" questions: *What? When? Where? Why? How?* Typically, these questions result in simple answers. For instance, when you ask someone, *"How are you?"* most people will reply with *"Fine."* Instead, try asking for a *story* as a way to encourage a fuller, richer response. Ask children to tell you a story about their feeling, thought, and/or experience. Everyone likes a story, and using the word "story" can also help a child feel less interrogated or put on the spot.

Children can also be taught to tell themselves stories about what they are dealing with, incorporating feeling words, concepts, and tools they're learning into their stories to help them get through a tough experience. This fosters self-talk and helps build resiliency; furthermore, it promotes self-help and self-care that lead to self-confidence.

6 **MISTAKES**
Everyone makes mistakes, and that's okay! This is what you want to communicate to the children you work with as they strive to learn about their feelings and how to express them. People may yell or say unkind words in the heat of the moment. The Kimochis® Way understands this and believes that everyone deserves a **redo**—the chance to stop and start again if they make a communication mistake. It's not about changing what is felt but about making another effort to communicate feelings more effectively.

7 **HARD-TO-HAVE FEELINGS**
Feelings can be put into two basic categories: feelings we like to have and feelings we do not like to have. Explain to children that *all* feelings are important and necessary. All feelings help us to learn and to grow, even the ones that make us feel bad and aren't easy to live with. Feelings are very powerful and can affect how we think and act, and they can make our bodies not feel good on the inside. We label this category of upset feelings "hard-to-have feelings." Talking about these feelings in this way helps children get some distance from tough emotions. This then allows them to develop ways to deal with these feelings and use communication tools to make things better for both themselves and others.

Kimochis®

Kimochis 5 Keys to Communication

1

Get someone's attention.
SEL TOOLS: *Eye contact, Communication Tap*

2

Use a talking voice.
SEL TOOLS: *Talking Voice, Fighting Voice, Serious Voice*

3

Use a talking face and body.
SEL TOOLS: *Talking Eyes, Fighting Eyes, Serious Eyes*

4

Choose helping words.
SEL TOOLS: *Helping vs Hurting Words, "Ouch"*

5

Redo hurtful moments.
SEL TOOLS: *Everyone Makes Mistakes, Kimochis Re-do*

Kimochis®

Kimochis 7 Keys to Communication

1

Get someone's attention.
SEL TOOLS: *Eye contact, Communication Tap*

2

Use a talking voice.
SEL TOOLS: *Talking Voice, Fighting Voice, Serious Voice*

3

Use a talking face and body.
SEL TOOLS: *Talking Eyes, Fighting Eyes, Serious Eyes*

4

Choose helping words.
SEL TOOLS: *Helping vs Hurting Words, "Ouch"*

5

Redo hurtful moments.
SEL TOOLS: *Everyone Makes Mistakes, Kimochis Re-do*

6

Be Kind and Let People Try Again
SEL TOOLS: *Second chances help make things better.*

7

Assume the Best
SEL TOOLS: *Train your brain to think the best. "Maybe they...." or "At least...."*

Kimochis®

Social-Emotional Learning (SEL) Vocabulary

KEY 🔑1	Get someone's attention: call their name, wait for eye contact, and give a communication tap, if necessary, before speaking.
Vocabulary Term	*Definition of Vocabulary Term*
Eye Contact:	Looking at others' eyes when listening and talking.
Communication Tap:	A light, gentle tap on the shoulder of another person as a way to get their attention.

KEY 🔑2	Use a talking tone of voice and volume in helpful ways instead of a fighting tone of voice.
Vocabulary Term	*Definition of Vocabulary Term*
Talking Voice:	A calm tone of voice, slightly slowed down, at an appropriate volume that conveys respect and self-control.
Fighting Voice:	A loud and hurtful tone of voice that conveys aggressiveness.
Serious Voice:	Slow, stretched speech that communicates that your message is important. Use a serious voice when you want to send an "I mean it" message without being mean.

Kimochis

Social-Emotional Learning (SEL) Vocabulary

KEY 3	Use helpful, not hurtful, facial expressions and body language, like a talking body and eyes and friendly signals.
Vocabulary Term	*Definition of Vocabulary Term*
Talking Body:	An open and relaxed body that conveys respect and self-control.
Talking Eyes:	Relaxed and calm eyes.
Fighting Eyes:	Squinty, mean eyes and a scary face.
Serious Eyes:	Wide eyes and raised eyebrows that communicate that what you are saying is important. Use serious eyes when you want to send an "I mean it" message without being mean.
Talking Hand:	Put your hand out palm up; use your other hand to tap your open palm; wait patiently for the person to return object; say thank you with eye contact when they do.
Friendly Signals:	Using gestures and words to convey friendliness: eye contact, a head nod, smile, wave, pat on the back.

KEY 4	Choose words that help rather than hurt (for example, "I feel mad because ..." instead of "I hate it when ...").
Vocabulary Term	*Definition of Vocabulary Term*
Helping Words:	Positive words that resolve feelings and conflicts.
Hurting Words:	Negative or loaded words that create upset feelings.
"Ouch":	Said in a soft voice with a hurt facial expression to let someone know in a gentle, shame-free way that they hurt your feelings.

Kimochis®

Social-Emotional Learning (SEL) Vocabulary

KEY 5	Be brave and redo hurtful moments when you make a communication mistake.
Vocabulary Term	*Definition of Vocabulary Term*
Own It:	Bravely apologizing for unkind words and actions and taking full responsibility with no excuses; pair with "Name it."
Name It:	(1) Describe exactly what you said or did that was not okay. (2) Explain yourself ("I get bossy when I feel cranky"). (3) Share a unique quality about yourself ("I talk really fast when I get excited").
Redo:	To begin again, using more positive words and actions.

KEY 6	Be kind and forgiving by letting others take a redo when they make a mistake.
Vocabulary Term	*Definition of Vocabulary Term*
Apologize:	To express regret for something said or done.
Forgive:	To let go of resentment, be kind, and let people try again.

KEY 7	Assume the best of others.
Vocabulary Term	*Definition of Vocabulary Term*
Assume the best:	Training your brain to think the best rather than assuming the worst about what others do and say.

Kimochis®

Make your own feelings!

What do your feelings look like?

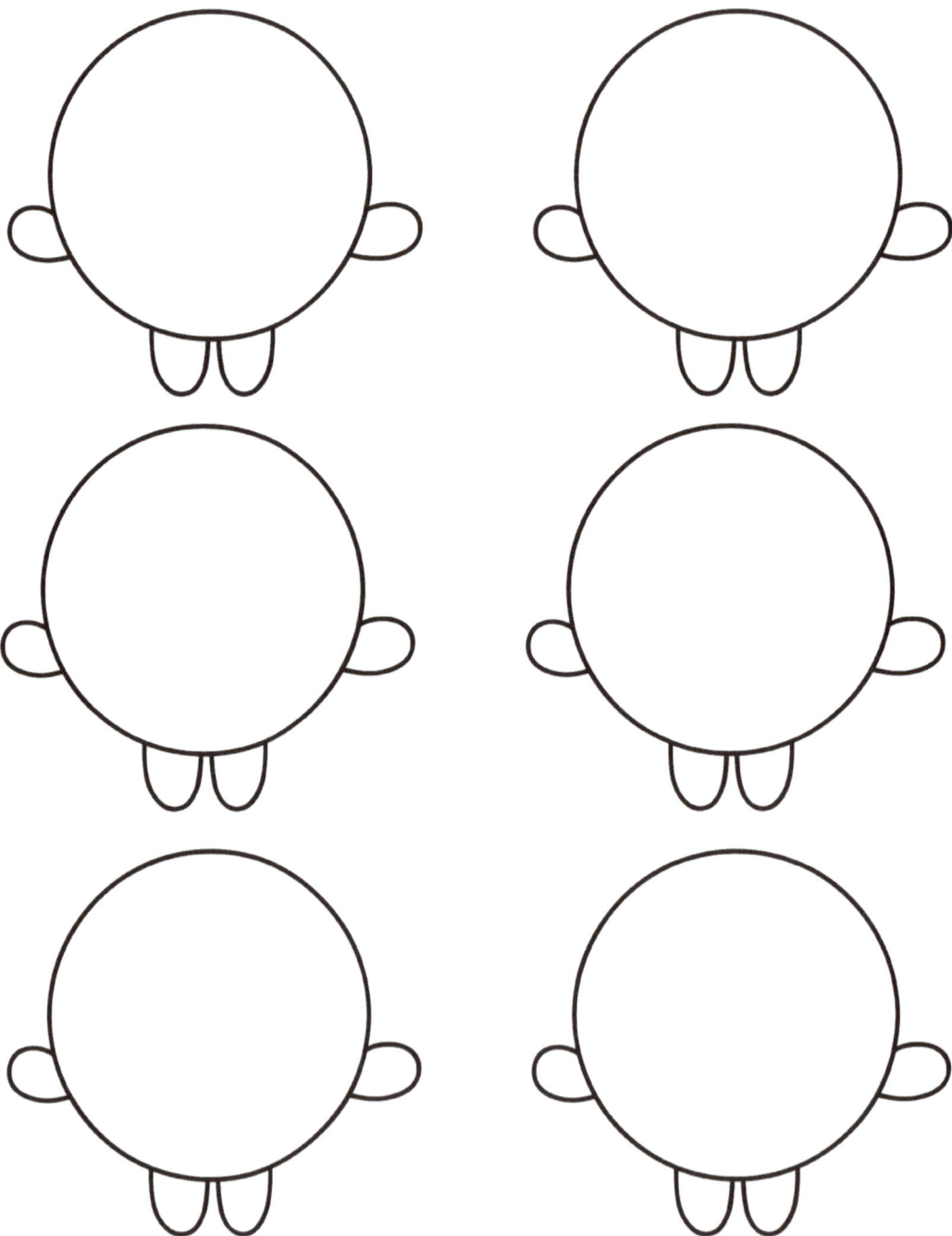

Kimochis®

Feelings Fuel Behavior
Worksheet

I'M	MAKE IT		I WANT TO			Tool
Feeling	Bigger	Smaller	Think	Do	Share	
Mad		✓		✓		Punch a pillow, Scream into a pillow until I feel less angry.

About the Authors

Ellen Pritchard Dodge, M.Ed., CCC-SLP
Speech-Language Pathologist & Kimochis® Educational Director

Ellen Pritchard Dodge is a recognized leader in character education and communication skills in the classroom who has published numerous books and articles in the area of social-emotional learning. She infuses her public speaking appearances with her passion for raising children's social and emotional intelligence as she applies her interactive workshop style and effective communication strategies. Ellen has taught extensively in public schools throughout Northern California, where her communication curriculum won a National Character Education award.

In collaboration with Dr. William Pollack, author of *Real Boys,* Ellen created academically and socially engaging classrooms for boys through the Supporting Our Sons organization. Since 2008, she has been the Education and Curriculum Director for Kimochis®.

In 2013, Ellen served on *Parenting* magazine's Editorial Advisory Board. In 2018, the California Speech-Language-Hearing Association bestowed its highest honor on Ellen, the Honors of the Association, for her significant contribution to the field of speech and language pathology and to the CSHA itself.

Ellen is the mother of three daughters and lives in Northern California, but she treasures her midwestern roots and her large extended family in Chicago.

Jill Kristal, Ph.D.
Licensed Clinical Psychologist & Kimochis® Certified Trainer

For 30+ years, Jill Kristal's work with children and adults has been guided by conversation, creativity, goal-directed play, and fun with purpose. Using a combination of psychotherapy, counseling, coaching, and education, she works to assist people in moving forward with their lives. Her humor and personal vignettes make her a sought-after speaker and writer on life transitions, parenting, and other mental health topics.

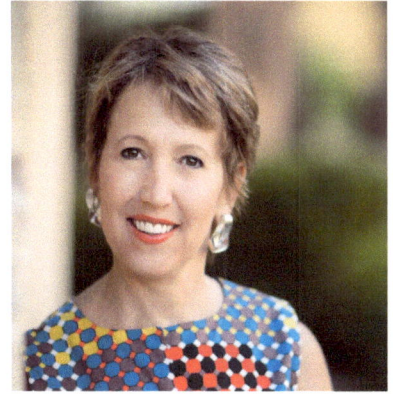

Jill lived for 12 years in London, England, where she served as Clinical Director of the American Counseling Center, an initiative of the U.S. Embassy. With two colleagues, she created Transitional Learning Curves and developed six interactive workbooks and games to guide relocating families through the process of transition that accompanies moving. Upon her return to the United States, Jill served as Special Education Coordinator at School Choice International. She is certified in EMDR, a trauma-based treatment approach. She currently has a private practice for children, teens, and adults in Westchester County, New York.

Upon being introduced to Kimochis® by a family she was working with, Jill instantly recognized the Kimochis® feeling pillows to be a concrete, hands-on, nonthreatening tool for helping children *and* adults improve their ability to experience and express their feelings. As a total Kimochis® enthusiast, Jill has introduced the Kimochis® characters and pillows to colleagues and has attended professional conferences with Bug and Hero in tow. Jill is presently working with Ellen Pritchard Dodge on materials to expand the applications of the Kimochis® product line in therapy.

Note to Readers

Please note that much thought, many hours, and significant effort went into the creation of this guide. It is intended for use by the mental health community with children and their families who can benefit from the Kimochis® therapeutic approach and strategies.

As such, no part of this guide may be reproduced, reprinted, copied, translated, stored in a retrieval system, or transmitted in any form without written permission of the authors.

Thank you for respecting our work.

www.ingramcontent.com/pod-product-compliance
Lightning Source LLC
Chambersburg PA
CBHW060859270326
41935CB00003B/32